Jokes and Riddles from A to Z

This Armada book belongs to:

_____

_____

_____

Jokes and Riddles from A to Z

Compiled by Bill Howard

with drawings by Graham Round

AN ARMADA ORIGINAL

Jokes & Riddles From A to Z was first
published in 1979 as an Armada Original
by Fontana Paperbacks, 14 St. James's Place,
London SW1A 1PS.

Printed in Great Britain by Love &
Malcomson Ltd., Brighton Road, Redhill,
Surrey.

ANGELS

Why is it fun to be an angel?
*Because when you get up to heaven you will have a high
old time.*

1st ANGEL: It's easy to see that Jones was a careful
motorist when he was on earth.
2nd ANGEL: What makes you say that?
1st ANGEL: Because now he's up here, he's asked to
be fitted with wing mirrors.

St. Peter was interviewing a fresh arrival when he noticed that he'd got a large bump on his head. 'How did you get that?' he asked.

'On the way up,' said the new arrival, 'I got hit by a jumbo-jet.'

JOAN: I think Elsie is an absolute angel.
PEGGY: Yes, you can tell by the way she harps on things.

ANIMALS

FATHER RABBIT: Can you keep my daughter in the manner to which she has been accustomed?
SUITOR RABBIT: Yes, sir! If I can marry her, I'll have the doe (*dough*).

Which animal has got wooden legs?
A timber wolf.

What sort of animals use nut-crackers?
Toothless squirrels.

Why is a horse like a cricket match?
Because it gets stopped by the rein (rain).

What did the hungry donkey say when he only had
    thistles to eat?
Thistle have to do.

What are the largest ants in the world?
Elephants.

How would you get rid of a white elephant?
Put it in a jumbo sale.

Why are sheep like pubs?
Because they are full of baas (bars).

Why did the ant-elope?
Nobody gnu.

What happened when two American stoats got married?
They became the United Stoats of America.

What did the bull say after he'd been to the china shop?
I've had a smashing time.

What's the difference between a kangaroo and a lumber-
   jack?
One hops and chews, the other chops and hews.

1st **W O R M** : Those two snails are having a nasty fight.
2nd **W O R M** : Leave 'em alone, and let them slug it out.

NATURAL HISTORY TEACHER: Can anyone tell me what sort of insect a slug is?

BOY: Yes, sir ... it's a snail with a housing problem.

What happened to the frog when it died?
It just croaked.

Which are the snootiest animals in the zoo?
Giraffes, because they look down on people.

What is a cheerful pachyderm?
A happy-potamus.

ARMY

Who are the shortest soldiers in the army?
The infantry, because they are foot-soldiers.

SERGEANT: Oi there, don't slouch, you're supposed to be marching. Pick up your feet!
SOLDIER: O.K., Sergeant, and where shall I put them —in my haversack, or just carry them in my hand?

1st SOLDIER: Our new C.O. rose from the ranks.
2nd SOLDIER: Yes, he used to be a taxi driver.

SALLY-ANN: And did you see the guards change when you were up in London?
MARY-LOU: No. When they saw I was looking they pulled down the blinds.

SERGEANT (*after drilling new recruit*): And what the dickens were you before you joined the army?
NEW RECRUIT: 'Appy, Sergeant.

RECRUITING SERGEANT: What's your name?
RECRUIT: Fish, sir.
RECRUITING SERGEANT: O.K. You can serve in a tank.

Why are army sergeants like dentists?
Because they are both good at drilling.

Why are N.C.O.s like zebras?
Because they both have stripes.

Why is a rifle like a lazy worker?
Because they can both get fired.

NIGHT SENTRY: Halt! Who goes there?
VOICE: Well I never! How did you know my name was Hugo?

ARTISTS

Which artist had an arresting personality?
Constable.

What sort of artist tries to put some money away for a rainy day?
A pavement artist.

TEACHER: What is pop-art?
BOY: That's what Dad says to Mum when he's going to pop-art for a quick one down the pub.

Why are painted portraits like a tin of sardines?
Because they are usually done in oils.

Why need artists never be short of money?
Because they can always draw a cheque.

1st ARTIST: Do you like painting people in the nude?
2nd ARTIST: Personally I like to paint with my clothes on.

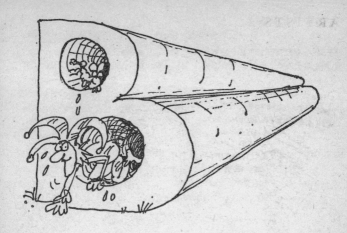

BAKERS

Why did the lazy man try to get a job with a baker?
*Because he thought it would be just the place for a good
   loaf.*

OLD LADY: What's that loaf up there on the shelf?
ASSISTANT: That's a tin loaf, madam.
OLD LADY: My teeth aren't what they used to be,
   so could you please find me something a bit softer?

Why did the baker's son decide to follow in his father's
   footsteps?
Because it was bred (bread) in the bone.

Why does a baker do his work?
Just for the dough.

What is another reason for a baker to do his work?
To earn an honest crust.

15

BARBERS

BARBER: And would you like to have something on the hair?
CUSTOMER: Well . . . I don't often bet, but when I do I usually have something on the greyhounds.

CUSTOMER (*on getting the bill*): That's a lot to pay for a haircut, after all, I'm nearly bald.
BARBER: I know, sir. It was the time taken to find it to cut which cost the money.

BARBER: I see your hair is beginning to abdicate at the top.
CUSTOMER: Abdicate?
BARBER: Yes, sir. It's giving up the crown.

BARBER (*to boy customer*): Who cut your hair last—was it your Mum?
BOY: Yes, she did it with a pudding basin.
BARBER: If she does it next time, will you tell her to use scissors?

MMM... RICE PUDDING

Did you hear about the ex-policeman who became a a barber? He cut hair very well, but when it came to shaving he couldn't help nicking his customers.

BIRDS

Why did the pigeon fly over the racecourse?
Because he wanted to have a flutter on the horses.

Where do all good turkeys go when they die?
To oven.

Why doesn't the owl mind being silent?
Because when he is, he doesn't give a hoot.

1st PIGEON TO 2nd PIGEON: Look! Down there's a railway station . . . let's fly over it, and do a bit of train spotting.

What happens before a bird grows up?
It grows down.

Why wouldn't the parrot talk to the Chinaman?
Because he only spoke pigeon English.

CANNIBALS

CANNIBAL CHIEF (*to his daughter*): Now you have reached the time to get married we must look around for an edible young bachelor.

Why should you never upset a cannibal?
Because if you do you might find yourself getting into hot water.

CANNIBAL MOTHER (*to teenage daughter*): If your poppa could see you now, he'd turn in his gravy.

1st CANNIBAL: Every time I eat a missionary I feel sick.
2nd CANNIBAL: That's because you can't keep a good man down.

1st CANNIBAL: How do you know our new missionary's been eaten?
2nd CANNIBAL: I've got inside information.

1st CANNIBAL: Have you tried the new take-away Chinese restaurant?
2nd CANNIBAL: No. When I got there they'd run out of Chinamen.

Some cannibals only eat mermaids on Friday. Others eat fish and chaps.

What is a cannibal's favourite kind of soup?
One with plenty of body in it.

After the wedding ceremony the assembled guests toasted the bride and groom. They were delicious.

A cannibal chief sent a message to the Missionary Society: *'Last missionary was delicious. Please send another. Tinned or fresh frozen will do.'*

CATS

How can you tell one sort of cat from another?
By referring to a catalogue.

BILLY: Have you heard the story about the Manx cat?
JOHNNY: No, what is it?
BILLY: There isn't one, because there's no tale (*tail*) to tell.

What does a cat rest its head on when it goes to sleep?
A caterpillar.

ITS
NOT
FAIR..

What happened when the young cat swallowed a penny?
There was money in the kitty.

What animal can you never trust?
A cheetah (cheater).

1st LADY: That's a nice fur coat you're wearing. What sort is it?
2nd LADY: I'm not sure, but every time I walk past a dog, the fur goes up at the back.

Overheard at bus stop: *A black-and-white cat crossed my path today. Ever since then my luck's been decidedly patchy.*

Why is a pole-cat a very aristocratic animal?
Because it is a member of 'high' society.

YOUR HIGH TEA M'LADY

WIFE (*calling down from bedroom*): Have you put the cat out?
HUSBAND: Yes . . . I'm afraid so. I've just trodden on his tail.

CIRCUSES

Why is a trampoline act a tricky way of earning a living?
Because it's full of ups and downs.

Why are tightrope-walkers like book-keepers?
Because they know how to balance.

Why is waiting on the telephone like doing a trapeze
act?
Because you have to hang on.

Why is an acrobat a useful person to know?
Because he is always capable of doing a good turn.

Why is an acrobat like a whisky glass?
Because they are both tumblers.

MAISIE: Why did you marry an acrobat, Mary?
MARY: Because he was head over heels in love with
me.

Why are contortionists thrifty people?
Because they can make both ends meet.

1st CIRCUS PERFORMER: I've just discovered
the tightrope-walker's secret.
2nd CIRCUS PERFORMER: How did you find out?
1st CIRCUS PERFORMER: By tapping his wire.

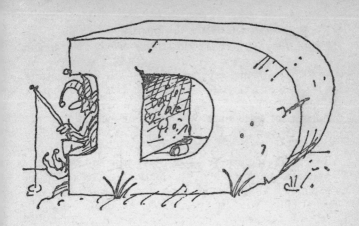

DENTISTS

Why are dentists artistic?
Because they are good at drawing teeth.

DENTIST: I'm afraid your front teeth will have to come out.
PATIENT: Oh, goodness me, parting with them is going to mean an awful wrench.

Why do dentists work in a curious way?
Because they sometimes start their work by stopping.

FRIEND: I suppose being a dentist is very interesting.
DENTIST: Yes, but the drilling gets a bit boring.

What sort of sweets are O.K. for your teeth?
Gums.

A new young dentist had a terrible struggle to extract a
   patient's teeth. When the patient came round he
   explained what a tough time it had been.
'Apart from your footprints on my chest,' said the
   patient, 'there's only one thing wrong. You've put
   my head back the wrong way round.'

DOCTORS

Why are doctors good-natured?
*Because they don't mind if you stick your tongue out
   at them.*

PATIENT: I keep getting a ringing in my ears.
DOCTOR: Don't worry. That means you are as sound
   as a bell.

PATIENT: I still feel very tired, doctor.
DOCTOR: Didn't you take those sleeping pills?
PATIENT: No. They looked so peaceful in the bottle that I didn't like to wake them up.

PATIENT: What shall I do to stop my nose from running?
DOCTOR: Next time it happens, put your foot out and try and trip it up.

DOCTOR (*after listening to a patient's numerous complaints*): Just a minute and I'll write something out for you.

PATIENT: Is it a prescription?

DOCTOR: No. It's a letter of introduction to the undertakers.

DOGS

During a bad snowstorm, a St. Bernard with a flask of brandy attached to his collar was sent out to search for a lost traveller. An hour later he came back with the brandy flask emptied and inside it a note: *Brandy excellent, will you please send a cigar.*

What's the difference between a whale-hunter and a happy dog?
One tags his whale, the other wags his tail.

TEACHER: What is meant by dogma?
PUPIL: A mother of pups.

VISITOR: Is your dog fond of children?
OWNER: Yes, but he does prefer biscuits and gravy.

A man took his dog back to the pet shop and complained that the dog made a shocking mess all over the house. 'You told me that it was house-trained,' he said. 'That's right, he is,' said the pet shop owner. 'He won't go anywhere else!'

1st MAN: Is that dog of yours a Scotch Terrier?
2nd MAN: That's right.
1st MAN: I thought so. Every time he sees me he tries to give me a nip.

JIM: Is that dog of yours a watch dog?
GEORGE: Yes.
JIM: Then please ask him to tell me the time.

You've heard of a flying fox, so what is a flying dog? *A Skye Terrier.*

Seen in a pet shop ... *'In the interest of dogs, hygiene is not permitted in this shop.'*

FRIEND: Your dog's got a funny bark.
OWNER: Yes, he's a dachshund, and speaks with a German accent.

Why was Lassie a famous dog in films?
Because she was always given the lead.

Which dog is the most expensive of them all?
A deerhound (dear hound).

ENTERTAINERS

1st COMIC: They say your wife's not a very good driver.
2nd COMIC: Yes. She's so bad that even the traffic lights go white when they see her coming!

1st COMIC: My new job means I've got dozens of people under me.
2nd COMIC: Are you a works manager?
1st COMIC: No, I keep the cemetery tidy.

1st COMIC: I'm always very careful to dry my hands thoroughly after washing them.
2nd COMIC: Why?
1st COMIC: If I don't, my nails will go rusty.

1st COMIC: What is the difference between you and a forger?
2nd COMIC: I give up.
1st COMIC: You try to make the funny, he tries to fake the money.

1st COMIC: I had a trip by the seaside yesterday.
2nd COMIC: I'm sorry to hear that. Did you hurt yourself?

EPITAPHS

Here lies a man who met his fate,
Because he put on too much weight.
To over-eating he was prone,
But now he's gained his final stone.

Here lies a chump who got no gain,
From jumping on a moving train.
Banana skins on platform seven,
Ensured his terminus was heaven.

This golfer here would swing his clubs,
Till time at last took toll.
Now in this grave below this stone,
He's reached his final hole.

Here rests the body of our M.P.,
Who promised lots for you and me.
His words his deeds did not fulfil,
And though he's dead, he's lying still.

Here lies a boy who played the fool,
When coming home one day from school.
He quite forgot his Highway Code,
What happened next he never knowed.

Here lies a boy who was a glutton,
And now he's dead, as dead as mutton.
To self-indulgence all he gave,
And with his teeth he dug his grave.

Old Tom is gone (too soon, alas!)
He tried to trace escaping gas.
With lighted match he braved the fates
Which blew him to the Pearly Gates.

ESKIMOS

If an Eskimo mum had a boy and a girl, what would
they be?
Blubber and sister.

What do they sing at an Eskimo's coming of age party?
Freeze a jolly good fellow (*For he's a jolly good fellow*).

1st ESKIMO BOY: Where does your mother come from?

2nd ESKIMO: Alaska.

1st ESKIMO BOY: Don't bother. I'll ask her myself.

What did the Eskimo say after he'd finished building his igloo?

Ours is an ice (a nice) house, ours is.

1st ESKIMO: That cough of yours is making you bark your head off.

2nd ESKIMO: Yes, I must admit that I'm a little husky.

What happened when the Eskimo girl fell out with her boyfriend?

She gave him the cold shoulder.

FISHING

WIFE: Good gracious, you look wet, what happened?
FISHERMAN HUSBAND: I lost my perch just as I was catching it.

Why are so many people mad about fishing?
Because it's an easy thing to get hooked on.

What fish is very musical?
A piano-tuna.

1st ANGLER: Get many bites today?
2nd ANGLER: Yes. Three fish and twenty mosquito.

MARY: Did you know Lucy liked fishing?
JANE: No, is she a keen angler?
MARY: Oh, she doesn't fish for fish, she fishes for compliments.

FOOTBALL

Why is Rugby football like a loaf of bread?
Because of its scrums (crumbs).

What's the difference between a good footballer and an industrious man?
One times his passes well, the other passes his time well.

MARY: Why does Harry spend so much time playing football?
SUSIE: Oh, he just does it for kicks.

CAPTAIN: You played a great game, Perkins.
PERKINS: I thought I played very badly.
CAPTAIN: You played a great game for the other side.

1st BOY: My dad's played at Wembley lots of times.
2nd BOY: I didn't know your dad was a footballer.
1st BOY: He isn't. He plays in the brass band that comes on the pitch before the match starts.

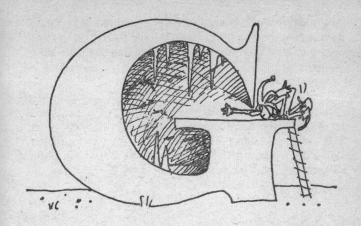

GEOGRAPHY

Why is Derbyshire a good place for pet dogs?
Because there you will find the Peak (Peke) District.

What happened when the Frenchman jumped off a
   bridge in Paris?
He went insane (in Seine).

Why is the Atlantic like an idea?
Because it's just a notion (an ocean).

What are government workers called in Seville?
Seville servants.

Why is Vesuvius like an irritable person?
Because from time to time it blows its top.

Where in France do houses have 'one up and one down'?
Toulouse (Two loos).

GHOSTS

1st GHOST: I see *The Phantom Killer's* on the telly tonight.
2nd GHOST: Yes, I saw it last week, and it nearly frightened the life into me.

What sort of song would a ghost sing?
A haunting melody.

Why are ghosts very simple things?
Because they can easily be seen through.

1st CYCLIST: My bike's always going wrong. I think it must have a jinx.
2nd CYCLIST: Yes, it's probably put a spook in your wheel.

GIRLS

JILL: I must say that Charlie is full of himself, isn't he?
LIL: Yeah . . . especially when he bites his nails.

POLLY: Last night I got a hot burning kiss from Henry.
MOLLY: Didn't think he was that sort.
POLLY: Well . . . he forgot to take the cigarette out his mouth.

CYNTHIA: I heard that it poured with rain on your sister's wedding day.

CLEMENTINE: Yes, even the bells were ringing (*wringing*) wet.

MAISIE: Lily's boyfriend is a real live wire.

ETHEL: He sure is . . . he's a proper shocker.

NORA: Bessie reminds me of a film star.

DORA: Really, which one?

NORA: Lassie.

LULU: Don't you think that Elsie overdoes it when she uses make-up?

VERONICA: Yes, she puts it on so thickly that for two minutes after she's stopped laughing her face is still smiling.

VAL: How are you getting on with teaching Harry to dance?

SAL: I'm hoping that soon he'll be able to stand on his own two feet instead of mine.

GOLFERS

NERVOUS GOLFER: Shall I need a driver for the next shot?

CADDY: Don't bother. You've only hit the ball five yards so we'll walk.

Why does a man become a golf pro?
In order to earn his bread and putter.

Why is a golf course like a Gruyere cheese?
Because they both have holes in them.

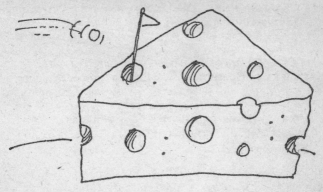

1st GOLFER: Did you hear Jones' language this morning? It was simply shocking.
2nd GOLFER: I should say it was. I thought he was playing on an eighteen-hole golf curse.

Why are golfers like cavemen?
Because they always walk around with clubs in their hands.

HISTORY

TEACHER: What happened when Drake was told an Armada was appearing?

BRIGHT PUPIL: He stopped playing bowls, and rushed out to buy one.

What is Dick Turpin, the highwayman, famous for?
He was one of the earliest road-users to cause traffic hold-ups.

Why did Henry the Eighth have so many wives?
Because he liked to chop and change.

What did Lot do when his wife got turned into a block of salt?
He put her in the cellar.

How did the inventor discover gunpowder?
It came to him in a flash.

HORSES

When is a horse like a bad egg?
When it's addled (saddled).

Why is a good-tempered horse not likely to be a good jumper?
Because it won't easily take offence (take a fence).

What letter comes straight from the horse's mouth?
The first letter, because it's an 'A' (a neigh).

1st TRAINER: That last race was a close finish. Did you think your horse had won?

2nd TRAINER: Yes, but when I saw the photo finish the answer was in the negative.

What sort of horse can you put your shirt on, and make sure you'll get it back?
A clothes horse.

What happened to Lady Godiva's horse when he saw
she'd got no clothes on?

It made him shy.

45

IDIOTS

FRIEND: Which side of the bed do you sleep on?
SIMPLETON: The top side, of course!

CUSTOMER: This is the second time I've called for my holiday snaps, and they're still not ready.
MANAGER: It's my new assistant. He's not very bright and is turning out to be a late developer.

CUSTOMER: I can't think of anything worse than this toad in the hole you've given me!
WAITER: I can. A frog in the throat.

1st IDIOT: What would you do if you found yourself locked out of the house?
2nd IDIOT: I'd keep on singing songs until I found one with the right key.

POLICEMAN: Why are you driving your car in reverse?
DAFT MOTORIST: Because I know the Highway Code backwards.

TEACHER: Hold out your hand, Jones. I'm going to give you the cane.

JONES: Oh, thank you, sir. What shall I do with it?

PASSENGER: How can I make sure the trains are running on time?

SILLY PORTER: Just before one comes in, put your watch on the railway line.

IDIOT: These socks you sold me have got holes in in them.

SHOPKEEPER: Of course. How do you think you're going to put them on without them?

1st IDIOT: I've discovered why large cars go quickly.

2nd IDIOT: Why's that?

1st IDIOT: Because they get a big boot behind.

POST OFFICE CLERK: Excuse me, but you've addressed this letter upside-down.

IDIOT: That's right. It's going to Australia.

INSECTS

Overheard at the watch repairer's: *This is a lousy clock. Yes indeed . . . it's full of ticks.*

1st OPERATIC SINGER: I thought you sang the Song of the Flea extremely well.

2nd SINGER: Yes, I must have done, all the people in the front row were scratching.

What did the mother bee say to the baby bee?
Don't be naughty, honey. Just beehive yourself while I comb your hair.

Did you hear about the glow-worm who got in a tizzy?
She didn't know whether she was coming or glowing (going).

1st WOODWORM: How's life these days?
2nd WOODWORM: Same as usual . . . boring.

What makes the letter 'T' so important to a stick insect?
Because without it, it would be a sick insect.

If a straight line is the shortest distance between two points, what is a bee line?
The shortest distance between two buzz (bus) stops.

What happens to a flea when it becomes really angry?
It gets hopping mad.

What happened when two lice moved to a new address?
They decided to give their friends a louse-warming party.

INVENTIONS

What happened when James Watt saw steam coming from the kettle?
He discovered it was time to make a nice cuppa.

What happened when the wheel was invented?
It caused a revolution.

TEACHER: What did Robert the Bruce do after he watched the spider climbing up and down?
PUPIL: He went and invented the yo-yo.

Why was the inventor of the safety match so pleased?
Because it was a striking success.

What happened when the steam-hammer was invented?
It made a great hit.

What was the name of the first mechanical man to be invented?
Frank N. Stein.

Who invented the first pen?
The Incas. (Inkers).

What kind of invention was the clock?
A timely one.

What happened to the discoverer of electricity?
He got a nasty shock.

JOBS

What is another name for a butcher's boy?
A chop assistant.

Why is a carpenter like an airman?
Because they both know a lot about planes.

51

What does a diver get paid if he works extra hours.
Undertime.

What is a press photographer?
A flash guy.

Did you hear about the girl who thought that when a
haggis was piped in it was done by a Scottish plumber?

What kind of person makes a good money-lender?
Someone who takes a lot of interest in his work.

Why did Moses have to be hidden quickly when he was
a baby?
Because it was a 'rush' job to save him.

EMPLOYMENT OFFICER: Here's a job with plenty
of good openings.
APPLICANT: What is it?
EMPLOYMENT OFFICER: Doorman at the Ritz
Hotel.

CUTHBERT: In his job my Dad's one of the high-ups.
CLARENCE: What does he do?
CUTHBERT: He's a steeplejack.

JIMMY: My Dad's a big time operator.
FRED: What sort of job is that?
JIMMY: He winds up Big Ben.

JUDGES

JUDGE: I've decided to give you a suspended sentence.
PRISONER: Thank you, your Honour.
JUDGE: Don't thank me, you're going to be hanged.

JUDGE: I'm going to give you a short sentence.
PRISONER: Thank you, your Honour.
JUDGE: Ten years, that is my decision.
PRISONER: Ten years! That's not a short sentence.
JUDGE: Yes it is—two words.

JUDGE (*to barrister*): Your client doesn't appear to take the charges very seriously.
BARRISTER: Well, he's a professional pick-pocket, and he is apt to take things rather lightly.

JUDGE (*to constable*): You say the prisoner is a sailor, and he hit a man over the head with a torch?

CONSTABLE: Yes, your Honour.

JUDGE: What is the charge?

CONSTABLE: It's a case of a salt and battery (*assault and battery*).

What did the judge say after he'd finished work?
It's been another trying day.

KIDS

Overheard at school:
Young Jones is a born leader. He's always the first away when school is over.

MOTHER: My Herbert certainly sticks to his hobby.
NEIGHBOUR: What's that?
MOTHER: Watching the telly. When it's on he's glued to the set.

MOTHER: When the new baby comes, do you want a baby brother or a baby sister?
LITTLE BOY: I'd sooner have a jelly baby.

HAMISH: Am I your closest chum?
HARRY: I think you must be . . . you never give me anything.

What kind of cake would most small boys not mind going without?
A cake of soap.

DAD: When I was your age I had lovely wavy hair.
SON (*looking at Dad's bald head*): Well, since then it's certainly waved you goodbye.

1st KID: My uncle was arrested the other day.
2nd KID: What happened?
1st KID: He went shopping after drawing ten pounds.
2nd KID: What's wrong with that?
1st KID: The drawing wasn't good enough. The shop spotted it was a forgery.

How did the boy feel after being caned?
Absolutely whacked.

KINGS

Why should a thoughtful king never be a fat one?
Because he would always be a'thinking (a thin king).

Why is a champion tennis player like a king?
Because he rules the court.

What English king had an heart transplant?
*Richard the First, because when he became a Crusader
he was known to have the heart of a lion.*

When the tide came up to King Canute
He wished they'd invented the Wellington boot.

What was King Alfred called after he had burnt the
cake?
Alfred the Grate.

Who was the greatest King never crowned?
King Kong.

Just before King Charles was executed he was allowed to make a final request, so he asked if he could take his pet spaniel for a walk around the block.

KNOCK KNOCK

Knock knock
Who's there?
Justin
Justin who?
Justin time for a cuppa.

Knock knock
Who's there?
Isadore
Isadore who?
Isadore not a door when it's ajar?

Knock knock
Who's there?
Alison
Alison who?
Alison Wonderland.

Knock knock
Who's there?
Ivor
Ivor who?
Ivor a message for you

Knock knock
Who's there?
Ivor
Ivor who?
Ivor good mind not to tell you.

Knock knock
Who's there?
Police
Police what?
Police let me in.

Knock knock
Who's there?
Percy
Percy who?
Persevere and you may find out

Knock knock
Who's there?
Jemima
Jemima who?
Jemima asking, but who lives here?

Knock knock
Who's there?
Bella
Bella who?
Bella no ringa, thatsa why I knocka!

Knock-knock
Who's there?
Solly.
Solly who?
Solly you been tloubled. Me makee mistakee.

Knock-knock
Who's there?
Godfrey.
Godfrey who?
Godfrey tickets for the theatre tonight?

Knock-knock
Who's there?
Theodore.
Theodore who?
Theodore is shut. Come down and let me in.

Knock-knock
Who's there?
Willoughby.
Willoughby who?
Willoughby be quick and open the door.

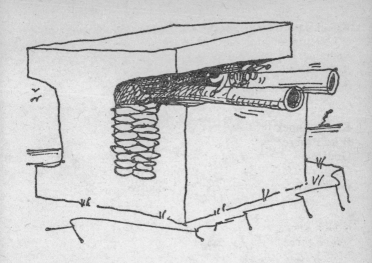

LANDLADIES

1st MAN: I wonder why these boarding house keepers are called *land*-ladies.
2nd MAN: Because they charge the earth.

1st WOMAN: What was the weather like on your holiday?
2nd WOMAN: It was so bad that every time the sun shone the landlady charged it up as an extra.

GUEST: Didn't you say that your boarding house was only a stone's throw from the sea?
LANDLADY: That's right. Just keep practising. You'll soon be able to throw it a quarter of a mile.

JIMMY: We're going to the same place next year for our holiday.
JOHNNY: Why?
JIMMY: Because Mum wants to see if the landlady has changed the tablecloth.

LANDLADY (*to enquirer*): Board and lodging will be twenty pounds for the week.

ENQUIRER: And how much for the strong?

MRS. JONES: All the boarding houses were full up when we went on holiday.

MRS. SMITH: But did you manage to get taken in?

MRS. JONES: Oh yes, well and truly, when we discovered what the bill was.

1st LOONY: Why are you standing in that bowl of
water?
2nd LOONY: Because the tablets I'm taking say 'To
be taken in water three times a day'.

BUS CONDUCTOR: Come down, there's no standing
on top of this bus.
LOONY: Why not?
BUS CONDUCTOR: Because it's a single decker.

1st LOONY: I got involved in a narrow squeak.
2nd LOONY: What was it?
1st LOONY: I trod on a thin mouse.

1st LOONY: Do you know what a laser is?
2nd LOONY: Yes, it's what a Chinaman shaves with.

LADY (*opening the door to visitor*): Why are you standing there with your socks and shoes in your hands?

LOONY VISITOR: You told me to make sure next time I came to wipe both my feet on your mat.

1st LOONY: Someone just asked me if I was something to do with the F.B.I.

2nd LOONY: Federal Bureau of Investigation?

1st LOONY: No. Feather-brained Idiot.

MOTORISTS

MOTORIST: When I bought this car you said it was rust free. The underneath's covered with it.
DEALER: That's right, the car's rust free. We didn't charge for it.

What's the best place for a motorist to get a nice cuppa?
At a 'T' junction.

Why is a car wheel like a lazy person?
Because it's always tyred (tired).

NEIGHBOUR: Why have you two 'L' signs on the back of your car?
MOTORIST: Oh, one's for the wife. She's learning to drive. The other's for her mother sitting behind—she's learning to be a back-seat driver.

ADVERT: *Chauffeur required. Would suit man or woman with plenty of drive.*

C

LADY (*to garage hand*): I've had this car three months, what sort of service will I be needing?

GARAGE HAND: Judging by the way you're driving, it'll soon be a burial one.

MOTORIST: I've just got a 'flat'.

GARAGE MECHANIC: You're lucky, I'm still waiting on the housing list.

1st MAN: How's your wife's driving now that she's taking lessons?

2nd MAN: Simply 'L'-ish (*hellish*).

JONES: Don't you find it a bit sticky travelling to town these days?

SMITH: Yes, it's jam all the way.

MUMS AND DADS

MUM: I bumped into Mrs. Smith today.

DAD: Was she pleased to see you?

MUM: Not very. We were both in our cars at the time.

DAD (*looking at the morning post*): I see Mrs. Jones has notified us of her change of address.

MUM: She's lucky. It's years since I've had a change of a dress.

DAD: Doctor says I've got to get rid of twenty pounds.

MUM: I can help you. Tomorrow I'll go out and buy some new clothes. That'll help to get rid of twenty pounds in no time.

BILLY: Mum thinks Dad's a real smasher.

JOHNNY: That's nice of her.

BILLY: Yes, that's why she never lets him do the washing up.

DAD: Hullo, dear, I've just brought a friend home for dinner.

MUM: That's fine. Put him in the deep freeze and we'll have him next week.

MUM: Shall I put the kettle on?

DAD: Don't bother. I like the dress you're wearing.

MUSICIANS

CHINESE VISITOR: I like velly much the flute.
HOST: And do you play it?
CHINESE VISITOR: Oh no, I eat it—apples, pears, bananas and all sorts of flute.

What's the difference between a music maker and a corpse?
One composes, the other decomposes.

Why is a guitar like a turkey being made ready for the oven?
They both have to be plucked.

MUSIC TEACHER: What does 'allegro' mean?
PUPIL: It's what a line of chorus girls make with their legs.

Why is a piano like an eye?
Because they are both closed when their lids are down.

1st BOY: I'd like to be able to play the cornet.
2nd BOY: You're a rum one. I'd rather lick it.

VICAR: What do you think of our village band?
LISTENER: I think it ought to be.
VICAR (*puzzled*): Ought to be what?
LISTENER: Banned.

ELSIE: Listen. I can hear the band playing 'The Men of Harlech'.
MARY: Who's winning?

POP FAN: Did you say that you learned to play the guitar in six easy lessons?
POP STAR: That's right. It was the three hundred ones that came afterwards which were the hard ones.

What brass instrument is like a potato?
The tuba (tuber).

What happened when the electric guitar was plugged into the lamp standard?
It played light music.

What is a pirate's favourite instrument?
The lute (loot).

NEWS

INQUIRER: I want to put an advertisement in your newspaper.

TELEPHONIST: Is it to go in the Small Ads, sir?

INQUIRER: Heavens, no. I want to sell an elephant.

REPORTER: I've just got news of a big scoop.

EDITOR: Splendid, what is it?

REPORTER: The local council have just bought a new mechanical shovel.

Asked how he made his money, Mr. Harry Kiri, the Japanese millionaire, said he just had a yen for that sort of thing.

It is reported that an income-tax inspector has successfully demonstrated to a blood-donor unit how to get blood out of a stone.

Mr. and Mrs. Jones and their son have just won first prize at the Nudists' Fancy Dress Ball. They went as the three bares (*bears*).

BILL: Anything interesting in the newspapers today?
FRED: Only fish and chips.

Do twins born in Holland speak double Dutch?

It is difficult to get an electrician to mend a fuse because to do so he has to re-fuse.

If you want to make money, screw up a five pound note, open it up and you will find it in creases (*increases*).

If you attended a skeleton's ball would you have a rattling good time?

If Guy Fawkes had succeeded in blowing up Parliament the House would have risen sooner than expected.

A tall building can be dangerous because it has a lot of flaws (floors) in it.

You can always tell a Pole because he has a wooden expression.

ODDITIES

POST OFFICE CLERK: What makes you think you should get a television licence for half price?
CUSTOMER: Because I've only got one eye.

1st LOONY: I find that time hangs heavily on my hands these days.
2nd LOONY: Then why don't you get a wristwatch instead of that grandfather clock you're wearing?

INQUIRER: Why are you standing on this railway bridge with a rod and line?

LOONY: I'm waiting to catch the next train.

PASSPORT OFFICER: Why are you standing on your head, sir?

TRAVELLER: Because some idiot has stuck my passport photograph in upside-down.

OPERATIONS

A man needed extensive plastic surgery. The only way the doctors could repair the damage was to graft on a piece of skin from his bottom. Asked how he felt, he said, 'Fine, except for one thing—when I get tired my face wants to sit down.'

What did the patient say to the anaesthetist?
Because of you, I've been considerably put out.

MATRON: The patient doesn't seem to be getting on very well with the new drip.
NURSE: No, I think the old doctor was much better.

SURGEON: How is the patient feeling after his heart operation?
ASSISTANT: Fine, except that he appears to have a double heartbeat.
SURGEON: Ah, that explains it! I wondered where my wristwatch had gone.

1st MAN: My wife's just had her fifth operation. I don't think the hospital surgeon likes her very much.
2nd MAN: Why?
1st MAN: He's always got his knife into her.

VISITOR: Glad your operation was a success, but you still appear to be a little pale.
PATIENT: I feel like one—I nearly kicked the bucket.

POLICEMEN

POLICEMAN (*to motorist*): I see that one of your tyres is bald.

MOTORIST: O.K. I'll see it gets some 'air.

OLD LADY: Constable, can you see me across the road?

CONSTABLE: I'll cross over in a minute, and if I can see you I'll wave.

Why is a policeman's job very tricky?
Because there are a lot of catches in his work.

What did the policeman say after booking a dozen motorists for illegal parking?
I've done a fine day's work.

When is a poor church collection like a policeman's helmet?
When it has just one copper in it.

What was the artistic policeman's favourite subject?
Drawing his truncheon.

What happens when the police take a burglar's fingerprints?
It creates a very bad impression.

POLICEMAN (*to motorist*): After the way I've seen you drive I'm going to introduce you to Eliza.
MOTORIST: Who's Eliza?
POLICEMAN: Breth-eliza (*breathalyser*).

Why are policemen strong?
Because they can hold up traffic with just one hand.

PSYCHIATRIST: Having listened to you, I find that what you need is a brain-wash.
PATIENT: Brain-wash, why?
PSYCHIATRIST: Because you have a dirty mind.

MOTHER: Jimmy just cannot stop biting nails.
PSYCHIATRIST: Nail-biting's not unusual for a small child.
MOTHER: What! Six-inch rusty ones . . . ?

PATIENT: I'd like to know what makes me flush so easily.
PSYCHIATRIST: Oh, flushing's just the result of a normal chain reaction.

Why is an expensive fur coat sometimes like a person who is in need of psychiatric treatment?
Because one may be of a minky kind, the other of a kinky mind.

PATIENT: I find it difficult to tell the truth.
PSYCHIATRIST: Don't worry. Once you get on the couch you'll find it very hard to lie on.

PATIENT: My trouble is I have a dual personality.
PSYCHIATRIST: Well, as this interview is strictly confidential, one of you had better wait outside.

PSYCHIATRIST: The best cure for you is shock treatment.

NEW PATIENT: O.K., Doc. You can begin it now by telling me how much it will cost.

PATIENT: May I lie down on the floor instead of the couch?

PSYCHIATRIST: Yes, of course, but why?

PATIENT: Because I want to discuss why my wife treats me like a doormat.

people just walk all over me....

PATIENT: The trouble is I can't help pulling ugly faces.

PSYCHIATRIST: That's not very serious.

PATIENT: It's not *my* face I want to pull . . . it's other people's.

QUESTIONS

What's the difference between . . .

A thunderclap and a lion with toothache?
*One may cause it to pour with rain. The other may
cause it to roar with pain.*

Someone who's just been bitten by a mosquito and
a runner waiting to race?
One's going to itch. The other is itching to go.

Between pack ice and a clothes brush?
One crushes boats. The other brushes coats.

Someone who enjoys rice pudding and a greedy shopkeeper?
One's a rice praiser. The other is a price raiser.

A water butt and a poor cricket fielder?
One catches the drops. The other drops the catches.

Between your parents and a tongue-tied lunatic?
One's mum and dad. The other's dumb and mad.

What's the difference between . . .

A jig-saw expert and a greedy boy?
One's a good puzzler, the other's a pud guzzler.

A hard-hitting batsman and a flea?
One's a ball smiter. The other's a small biter.

An ornithologist and a bad speller?
One's a bird watcher. The other's a word botcher.

The end of a queue and a letter box?
One makes the tail. The other takes the mail.

What's the difference between . . .

A sunbather and someone who lives in the Sahara?
*One gets tanned by the sun. The other gets sand by
the ton.*

QUICKIES

A twenty-stone girl got engaged to a thirty-stone man.
They planned to have a big wedding.

What would you see from the top of the Eiffel Tower?
An eyeful.

Did you hear the story about the dust-cart?
It was a load of rubbish.

What's a juggernaut?
An empty beer mug (a jug of naught).

MARY: Mabel went to a beauty parlour and had her
face lifted last week.
LUCY: Good heavens! Who'd want to steal a face like
that?

A boy bought a wristwatch, and promised to pay for it later.
He got it on tick.

GREEDY BOY: I got through a jar of jam today.
2nd BOY: From your size it must have been a very tight squeeze.

Newton discovered gravity when an apple hit him on the head.
The discovery shook him to the core.

1st GIRL: Don't you think Lulu's got a sweet face?
2nd GIRL: Yes indeed, just like a humbug.

GIRL: I wouldn't marry you if you were the last person on earth.
BOY: If I were, you wouldn't be here.

What did the jester have for dinner?
Quips with everything.

Why is a Viking like a cavalry officer?
Because he's a Norseman (an 'orseman).

What did the penny say when it got stuck in the slot?
Money's tight these days.

What sort of monkey has a sweet tooth?
A meringue-outang.

1st MAN: Do you like working on the railways?
2nd MAN: It certainly has its points.

What did the dry biscuit say to the almond?
You're nuts and we're crackers.

1st IRISHMAN: I'm Malone.
2nd IRISHMAN: For sure, 'tis aisy to see you're by yourself, since nobody else is wid yer.

What is oil before it is discovered?
A well-kept secret.

BOSS: Your socks are full of holes.
CLERK: I know, sir, it's my wife's fault. She doesn't give a darn.

JIMMY: There's one thing I'm an absolute sucker for.
JOHNNY: What's that?
JIMMY: A boiled sweet.

1st MAN: Does your wife cook best by gas or electricity?
2nd MAN: Don't know. I've never tried to cook her.

Did you hear about the anarchist who sold explosives?
He made a bomb.

MAN (*at gate*): Does your dog bite strangers?
OWNER: Only when he doesn't know them.

1st COMIC: Monty the Midget has applied for a job as a circus dwarf.
2nd COMIC: Well, at least he ought to get placed on the short list.

1st COMIC: Do you know what most gardeners don't like to grow?
2nd COMIC: Well, what don't they like to grow?
1st COMIC: Old, of course.

1st COMIC: And how is that dear wife of yours?
2nd COMIC: Very. She's just got me to buy her a fur coat.

1st COMIC: Why are a fat man's braces like a bad traffic jam?
2nd COMIC: Why are a fat man's braces like a bad traffic jam?
1st COMIC: Because they are both big hold-ups.

1st COMIC: We're going to call our new house 'The Millstone'.
2nd COMIC: Why?
1st COMIC: Because for the next twenty-five years the mortgage is going to be one round our necks.

RIB-TICKLERS

TEACHER: Does any boy know what C.I.D. stands for?

BOY: Coppers in disguise, miss.

INSURANCE AGENT: You want one of our Now and Later policies?

CUSTOMER: What sort of one is that?

INSURANCE AGENT: All-risks. While you're in this world it's a life insurance policy. In the next you're insured against fire.

CANNIBAL MOTHER (*to son*): Just because your father was tough when he was alive, that's no reason now to leave him on the side of your plate.

OPTICIAN: You'll be needing a pair of glasses, Mr. McTavish.

OLD JOCK: I canna afford a whole pair. Just gie me a monocle to be going on with.

LULU: Ethel's brother is going to be a chef.

MARY: He should do well, then. Whatever he does he makes a proper meal of it.

What's another name for a silly monkey?
A chumpanzee.

RIDDLES

When does a wooden floor feel cold?
When it is parquet (parky).

Why are scales like roadmaps?
Because they indicate the 'weigh' (way).

What's the difference between a buyer at a supermarket and the tide?
One shops at the store, the other stops at the shore.

Why is Madame Tussaud's an uncomfortable place to visit?
Because you are bound to meet with lots of wax (whacks).

Why is an M.P. like someone who queues for the cinema?
Because he stands in order to get a seat.

What is the best food to eat if you want to be strong?
Mussles and brawn (muscles and brawn).

What is the difference between a coyote and a flea?
One howls on the prairie, the other prowls on the hairy.

Why is a postage stamp like a very precise man?
Because they both stick to the letter.

What three letters does a wise man carry around with him?
A.Y.Z. (A wise head).

What is a cheerful flea?
A hop-tomist.

Why are first-class footballers like accomplished musicians?
Because they are very good players.

Why is a billiards hall a good place to go to get well?
Because there you will come across some good cuers (cures).

What are the warmest months of the year?
September, November and December, because they all have embers in them.

Why are postmen very learned people?
Because they are men of letters.

Why is 4,840 square yards like a bad tooth?
Because it is an acre (acher)

How do you know fishmongers don't mind filleting fish?
Because they make no bones about it.

What kind of clothes do judges and barristers wear?
Law-suits.

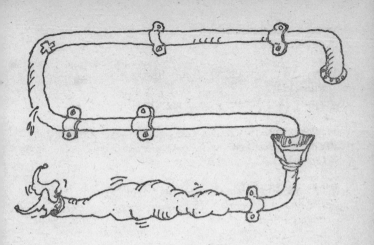

SILLYCISMS

ABANDON: What a big fat cigar has.

ADORE: Something you walk through.

BALL: Make a lot of noise.

BARBECUE: Line up for a hair cut.

BERET: Cover up.

BUOYANT: Brother of a sister ant.

DOCTRINAIRE: Flying doctor.

EMULATE: Dead emu.

HATCHET: What a bird tries to do when it sits on an egg.

KNAPSACK: Sleeping bag.

KNICKERS: Policemen.

LESSON: Result of taking some clothes off.

MINIMUM: Little mother.

GREENGROCER: Yes, madam, they're lovely tomatoes, they come from the Canaries.
CUSTOMER: Funny, I always thought they were grown, not laid.

Why is a cash register like someone who can't pay his bills?
Because it is pressed for money.

What did the customer say when told that the price of candles had doubled?
It's candleous (scandalous).

CUSTOMER: You said that this simple gadget was absolutely foolproof. I can't see how to use it.
SHOPKEEPER: Then it's what it says it is. It proves you're a fool!

A man went into a shoe repair shop and said to the new assistant, 'I want these shoes soled by this afternoon.' When he returned, he said, 'What about my shoes? I left them to be soled this morning.' 'Here's 50 pence,' said the assistant. 'I sold them almost as soon as you left the shop.'

ELDERLY SPINSTER: Is this the mail-order department?

SUPERVISOR: Yes, that's right, madam.

ELDERLY SPINSTER: Good! I'd like to order one, six foot tall, blue eyes, curly hair, and good at washing up.

Conversation overheard in a store:
'*You must have paid the earth for that.*'
'*No, I got it dirt cheap!*'

Did you hear about the little girl who thought her manx cat had lost its tail, and took it to the local retail store for a new one?

CUSTOMER: What's that meat hanging up in your shop?
BUTCHER: That, madam, is venison.
CUSTOMER: It seems very expensive.
BUTCHER: Of course it is, madam, because it's deer (*dear*).

What's the difference between the business of a removal firm, and a shop that sells notepaper?
One's moving, the other's stationary (stationery).

CUSTOMER: Those strawberries look as if they were picked weeks ago, yet your notice says 'Fresh Today'.
SHOPKEEPER: That's right. The notice *is* fresh today. I've only just written it out.

D

After eating a five-course meal, a diner called the waiter over and congratulated him.

'I'd like to finish with a brandy and some detergent,' he said. The waiter looked puzzled until the diner explained. 'You'll need the brandy when I tell you that I need the detergent to wash up with. I haven't any money to pay the bill!'

A ship cruising in the South Seas picked up a bottle in which there was a message that read: *'Jock McTavish shipwrecked on desert island. Latitude 50 deg. N. Longtitude 35 deg. S. Finder please rescue. Keep bottle. Three pence to come on it.'*

The businessman was checking out of the large hotel after a short stay. He was amazed when he was presented with his bill. 'A hundred pounds for two nights?' he exclaimed. 'Impossible!' 'Well, sir,' said the receptionist, 'you must remember that this is a five star hotel.' 'Five stars,' said the man. 'No wonder the bill is astronomical.'

After being beaten 10 nil, the home team trooped dejectedly back to the dressing room. 'Cheer up lads, it might have been worse,' said their trainer. 'At least you won something, even if it was only the toss.'

A new arrival, about to enter hospital, saw two white-coated doctors searching the flower beds. 'Excuse me,' he said, 'have you lost something?' 'No,' replied one of the doctors. 'We're doing a heart-transplant for an income tax inspector and want to find a suitable stone.'

A witch-doctor was initiating a young native into the art of witchcraft.
'Watch closely what I do,' said the witch-doctor, 'then voo-doo the same as I do.'

Two women were discussing their slimming diets.
'Don't you find it hard to have to go without sugar?' said one. 'No,' replied the other. 'When I think about it a lump just comes into my throat.'

Mrs. Jones didn't get on at all well with her husband. 'Why don't you give him the soft-soap treatment?' said Mrs. Smith. 'I've tried that,' said Mrs. Jones. 'Unfortunately he spotted it at the top of the stairs.'

The man walked into the baker's shop and said, 'I'd like a bath bun, please.' 'Certainly, sir,' replied the assistant. 'Anything else?' 'Yes,' said the man. 'I'll have a sponge to go with it.'

Two pick-pockets were discussing business.
'Did you have any luck over the weekend?' asked one.
'No,' the other replied. 'I spent it at a nudist camp.'

TEACHERS

TEACHER: If you keep on getting things wrong, Jones, I can't see much of a future for you.
BOY: Don't worry, sir . . . I want to be a weather forecaster.

MUSIC TEACHER: Is there anything special you'd like to be able to play?
BOY: Yes, sir . . . truant.

TEACHER: What is a myth?
BOY (*with a lisp*): Thome-one who ithn't a mithith.

TEACHER: What is a boycott?
PUPIL: A place where a baby boy sleeps.

TEACHER: What is the Lord's prayer?
BOY: For fine weather, sir, when they're playing cricket there.

Why are teachers rather special?
Because they are usually in a class of their own.

When a school teacher closes his eyes, why should he remind you of an empty classroom?
Because there are no pupils to see.

1st BOY: I wish we could sell our teacher.
2nd BOY: Why?
1st BOY: Because I read that at auctions Old Masters are fetching big prices.

TELEVISION

What sort of people want to go on the telly?
Those who like being in the picture.

MRS. JONES: We've had the telly for a month, and we've only switched it on once.
MRS. SMITH: That's not much.
MRS. JONES: Don't know about that, we haven't switched it off at all.

HUSBAND: Anything good on the telly tonight?
WIFE: Only your dinner. I've put it on the top of the set to keep warm.

RECRUITING SERGEANT: What's your religion, R.C. or C of E?
NEW RECRUIT: Neither, Sergeant, but sometimes the B.B.C. and sometimes I.T.V.

UNDERTAKERS

1st UNDERTAKER: How's business?
2nd UNDERTAKER: Same as usual . . . dead.

Where does an undertaker conduct his business?
In the box office.

What is a dead line?
A funeral procession.

What's another name for a coffin?
A snuff box.

How can you tell an undertaker?
By his grave manner.

How do you get through to the police in Australia?
Dial 666.

What's the difference between a simpleton and a Welsh Rarebit?
One's easy to cheat. The other's cheesy to eat.

1st BOY: My dad's just cured himself of dandruff.
2nd BOY: How?
1st BOY: He's gone completely bald.

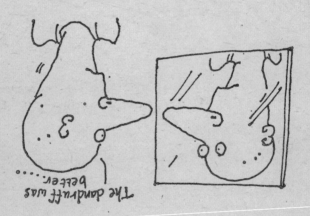

The dandruff was better....

1st CANNIBAL: How did the new missionary go down?
2nd CANNIBAL: Fine. We've ordered another one for Christmas.

What is double glazing?
A man with glasses who has had too much to drink.

Why are goal-keepers thrifty?
Because saving is their job.

1st B O Y : Don't you find that older people grumble a lot?

2nd B O Y : That's why they're called groan-ups.

Why did the tight-rope walker decide to give up?
Because his performance began to fall off.

VAMPIRES

Why are vampires really simple-minded?
Because they are known to be suckers.

What did the polite vampire say to his dentist after being
treated?
Fangs very much.

Why are vampires crazy?
Because they are often bats.

What is a vampire's favourite fruit?
A blood orange.

1st VAMPIRE: How's business?
2nd VAMPIRE: Rotten. I've had a letter today from my manager, and he says I'm overdrawn fifty pints at the blood bank.

TEACHER (*taking biology class*): What is a blood count?
PUPIL: Count Dracula.

VICARS

SUNDAY SCHOOL TEACHER: And what is the Holy See of Rome?
BOY: It's when the Pope looks at himself in the mirror.

VICAR (*discussing Church architecture*): What is a gargoyle?
CHOIRBOY: It's something you wash your throat with when it's sore.

1st CHURCHMAN (*talking about the changing fashions of the day*): I will say it's made quite a change to the collection.
2nd CHURCHMAN: Yes, I'd noticed it too. Since zips came in we get fewer buttons on the plate.

1st CHURCHGOER: I must say that the new vicar gave a thoroughly rousing finish to his first sermon.
2nd CHURCHGOER: Yes, I've never seen so many of the congregation wake up so quickly.

Why does a bishop sometimes keep doubtful company? *When he walks around with a crook.*

WAITERS

Why are waiters always willing to learn?
Because they are ready to take tips from people.

Why did the waiter look grumpy?
Because he had a chip on his shoulder.

Why are waiters good at sums?
Because they know their tables.

What is a representative of the Waiters' Union called?
A chop steward.

WAITER: Would you like to try some idiot soup, sir?
CUSTOMER: What's idiot soup?
WAITER: Thick soup.

DINER: What's wrong with this table, it's wobbling all over the place.
WAITER: It's the last customer's fault. He spilt a bottle of wine over it, and it's still drunk.

WAITER: Yes, sir. You can have anything you see on the menu.
CUSTOMER: O.K. I'll settle for the dirty fingerprints, grease marks, and gravy stains, in that order.

WAITER: The ten per cent was for service, sir.
CUSTOMER: It wasn't much in evidence.
WAITER: In this place, sir, it's secret service.

WAITER: Would you like a little wine with your dinner?
CUSTOMER: No thanks, if the dinner's no good, I'll do the whining after dining.

CUSTOMER: May I have the bill, waiter?
WAITER: But you've only just started to eat!
CUSTOMER: It's for my wife. She needs a bill to peck at her food.

IRATE CUSTOMER: This steak is awful. Bring me the manager.
WAITER: Sorry, sir, he's not on the menu.

CUSTOMER: This chicken's a battery hen.
WAITER: How can you tell that, sir?
CUSTOMER: From the taste. It's shocking.

WAITER (*to customer*): And after the steak what will you have to follow?

CUSTOMER: If it's anything like the one I had last week it'll be indigestion.

WHATS AND WHYS

What butterfly is like a Russian Naval Commander?
A Red Admiral.

What does one and one make in Ireland?
An Irish stew (two).

What did the Vikings use to keep in touch with one another?
The Norse code.

IT'S THE DOTS I CAN'T GET THE HANG OF!!

What's the difference between a good marksman and a violin case?
One finds the middle, the other minds the fiddle.

Why is an underground coal miner like a beautician?
Because they are both face workers.

What happened to the cannibals when they ate a comedian?
They had a feast of fun.

What's a bikini?
A space suit.

Why is a dollar millionaire an intelligent fellow?
Because he has a lot of cents (sense).

Why is a river a handy place for getting money?
Because there is a bank on either side.

Why is a sleeping baby like a hijack?
Because it's a kid-napping.

Why were Elijah's parents good business people?
Because between them they made a prophet (profit).

What kind of dance do prisoners do when exercising in the yard?
The quadrille (quad drill).

Why are missionaries popular with cannibals?
Because they go down very well with them.

What's the difference between an angler and a lazy
   schoolboy?
One baits his hooks, the other hates his books.

What happens to people who slim?
They have a thin time.

What did the egg say to the egg whisk?
I know when I'm beaten.

What cups can't be drank out of?
Buttercups and hiccups.

Why do nudists have plenty of time to spare?
Because they appear to have nothing on.

What did the violin say to the harp?
May I string along with you?

What did the harp reply to the violin?
I'd be harpy if you would.

What's another name for a sugar daddy?
A lolly-pop.

Why do two fivers make a singer?
Because together they make a tenner (tenor).

What's the difference between a Peeping Tom and someone who has just got out of the bath?
One is rude and nosy. The other's nude and rosy.

What's the difference between an orchestral conductor
and an oven?
One makes the beat. The other bakes the meat.

What's the difference between an ace tennis player and
a bully?
One smashes the ball. The other bashes the small.

Why did the man ring up the dentist?
Because he was simply aching to meet him.

Why are sea captains always on their toes?
Because their training makes them good skippers.

What is a witch when she's travelling on her broom?
A flying sorcerer.

Did you hear about the witch who couldn't write a
   decent letter?
She just couldn't spell properly.

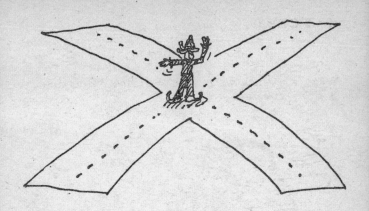

XMAS

What will happen to you at Christmas?
Yule be happy.

What did the fireman's wife find on Christmas day?
A ladder in her stocking.

How many chimneys does Father Christmas have to get down?
He has to get down stacks.

I think he's got it wrong again....

What did the woodman's wife say to him one day?
There aren't many chopping days to go before Christmas.

What did Father Christmas's wife say during a thunderstorm?
Come to the window and look at the rain dear (reindeer).

YARNS

Angus's son was going to London. 'Father,' he said. 'I'll be needing a wee bit of money.' So Angus took out a ten pound note and a pair of scissors, and, cutting off the corner of the note, remarked, 'There's yer wee bit of money, lad . . .'

Two Red Indians were watching some distant smoke-signals. When the signals were finished one Indian turned to the other and said, 'We shall have to do something about Sitting-Bull. His spelling is simply awful.'

The pub beer wasn't too good, and finally one of the customers complained. 'If this beer had a head on it,' he said, 'it would hang it in shame.'

'I hear,' said Mrs. Jones to Mrs. Smith, 'you've got a model husband.' 'True,' said Mrs. Smith, 'but unfortunately he's not a working model.'

The foreman complained to the boss that the navvies had gone on strike because of the new mechanical shovel. 'What's wrong with it?' he asked. 'The men,' said the foreman, 'say that it's too dangerous to lean on.'

Two men were discussing their wedding day experiences. Said one, 'I shall never forget mine, I got a terrible fright.'
'What happened?' said the other.
'Nothing,' replied the first. 'I married her.'

After making a purchase in a local shop, McDougal took out his purse to pay. He fumbled around for a time then looked up and said, 'Please, miss, can ye give ma change for a moth?'

Jones was late for work, and the boss asked for an explanation. 'I'm sorry, sir,' said Jones, 'but I got out of a sick bed to get here.' 'I'm sorry to hear that,' said the boss. 'What's wrong with you?' 'There's nothing wrong with me, boss,' said Jones. 'It's the bed that's sick. One of its legs got broken.'

'It's a long time since I had a square meal, lady,' whined the tramp. 'Hold on a minute,' said the lady. 'If it's a square meal you want I'll go and get you a large dog biscuit.'

The circus giant was hard up and asked the dwarf to lend him a pound until pay day. 'I'd love to,' said the circus dwarf, 'but as usual I'm terribly short.'

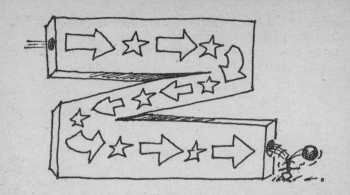

ZOOS

What did the keeper see when the elephant squirted water from his trunk?
A jumbo jet.

LADY PASSENGER (*to bus conductor*): Excuse me, am I all right for the Regent's Park Zoo?
CONDUCTOR: By the look of you, probably yes . . . but I'm only a bus conductor not a zoologist.

VISITOR (*in reptile house*): Where have all the adders gone?
KEEPER: They're helping out in the accounts department because the computer's broken down.

WIFE (*at the zoo*): That baby grizzly reminds me of our sitting room carpet.
HUSBAND: How's that?
WIFE: It looks a little bare (*bear*) to me.

What happened when the elephant died at the zoo?
They decided to bury it . . . but it was a huge undertaking.

HERE'S THE FINISH OF THIS FUN—
EVERYTHING'S BEEN Z AND DONE!

Armada Quiz Books

Boost your brain power and have hours of puzzling
fun solving the hundreds of quizzes in these exciting
Armada quiz books.

Armada Horse & Pony Quiz Book
by Charlotte Popescu

Armada Football Quiz Book
by Gordon Jeffery

The New Armada TV Quiz Book
by Peter Eldin

The Armada Animal Quiz Book
by Deborah Holder

The Great British Quiz Book
by Jonathan Clements

The Armada Round The World Quiz Book
by Yasmin Mottahedin

The Armada Zoo Quiz Book
by Gillian Standring

Armada

CAPTAIN ARMADA

has a whole shipload of exciting books for you

Here are just some of the best-selling titles that Armada has to offer:

- ☒ **Armada Quiz & Puzzle Book 4** Doris Dickens & Mary Danby 50p
- ☒ **The New Armada TV Quiz Book** Peter Eldin 50p
- ☒ **The Armada Animal Quiz Book** Deborah Holder 45p
- ☒ **The 14th Armada Crossword Book** Robert Newton 50p
- ☒ **The 2nd Armada Book of Fun** Mary Danby 40p
- ☒ **The Armada Zoo Quiz Book** Gillian Standring 45p
- ☒ **Captain Cobwebb** Gordon Boshell 40p
- ☒ **Spy in Space** Patrick Moore 45p
- ☒ **William—Again** Richmal Crompton 45p
- ☒ **Make Your Own Costumes and Disguises** Hal Danby 45p
- ☒ **The 2nd Armada Book of Limericks** Mary Danby 50p

Armadas are available in bookshops and newsagents, but can also be ordered by post.

HOW TO ORDER

ARMADA BOOKS, Cash Sales Dept., GPO Box 29, Douglas, Isle of Man, British Isles. Please send purchase price of book plus postage, as follows:—

    1—4 Books .... 8p per copy
    5 Books or more .... no further charge
    25 Books sent post free within U.K.

Overseas Customers

    1 Book: 10p. Additional books 5p per copy

NAME (Block letters)

ADDRESS